This coloring book is created by :

Mohamed Amine Artiba

Copyright 2021

If you are intrested in our creations
you can visit the pintrest
by copy this link and open it your browser

https://www.pinterest.com/luizotaku2005/
_saved/

Have a fun time :)

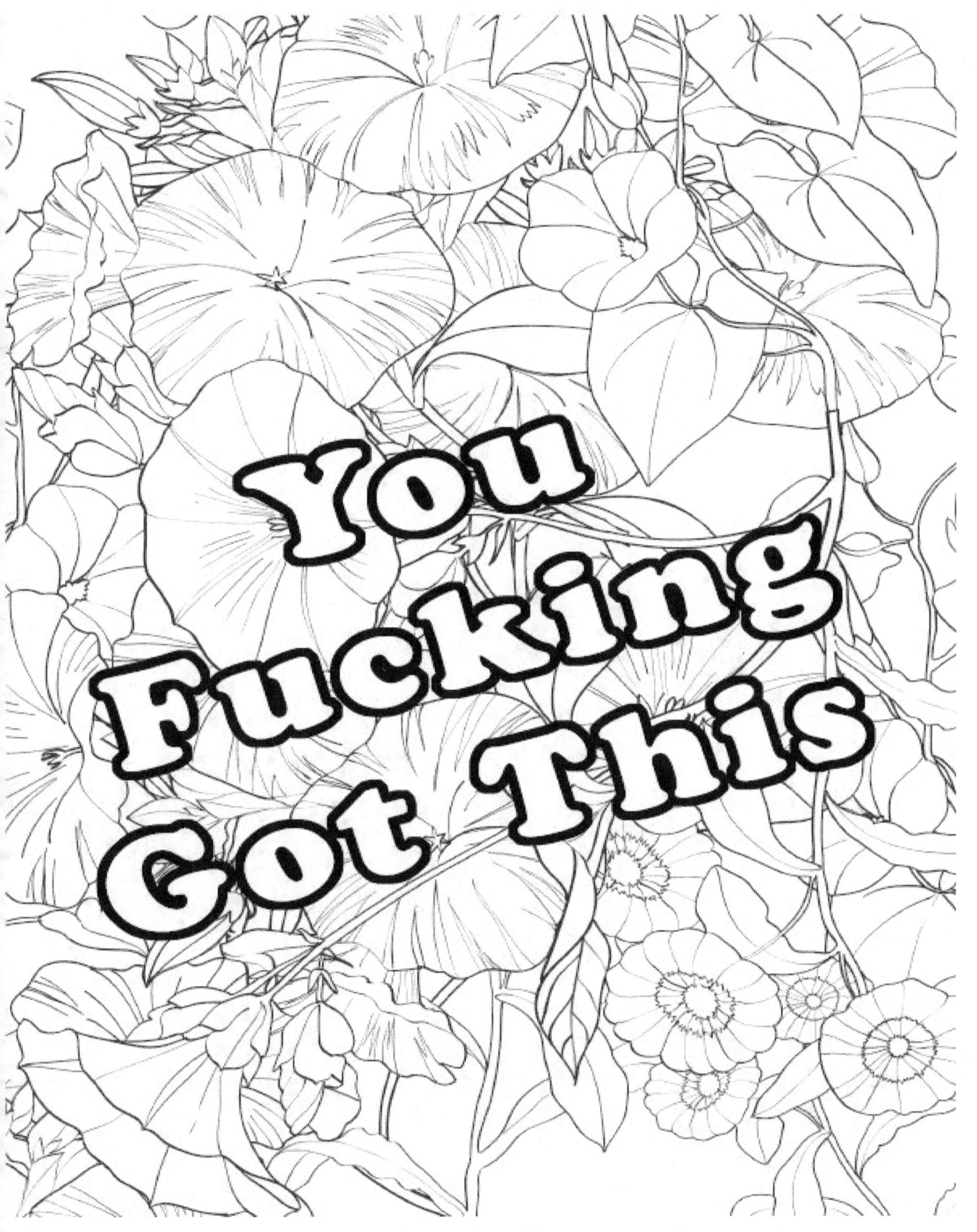

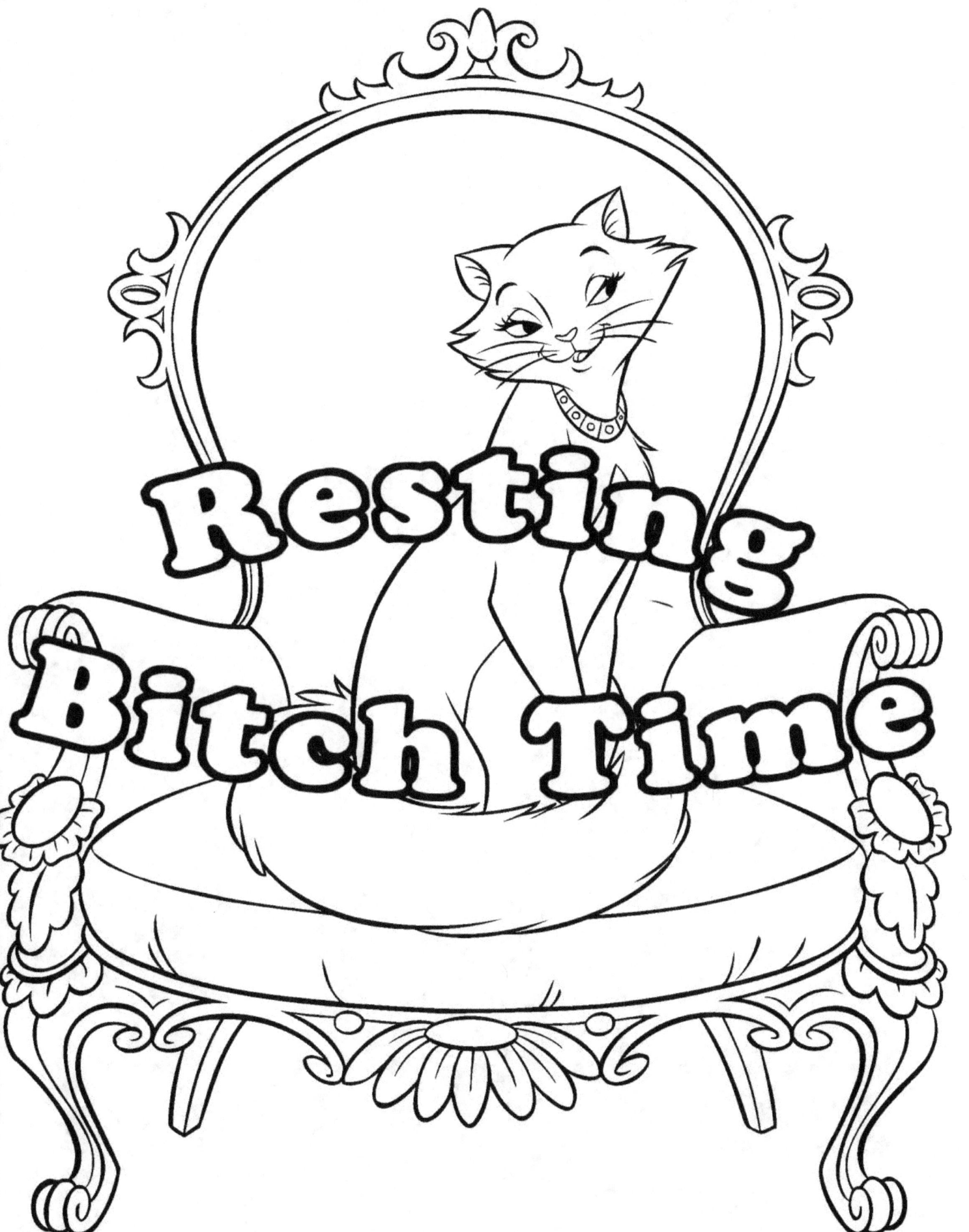

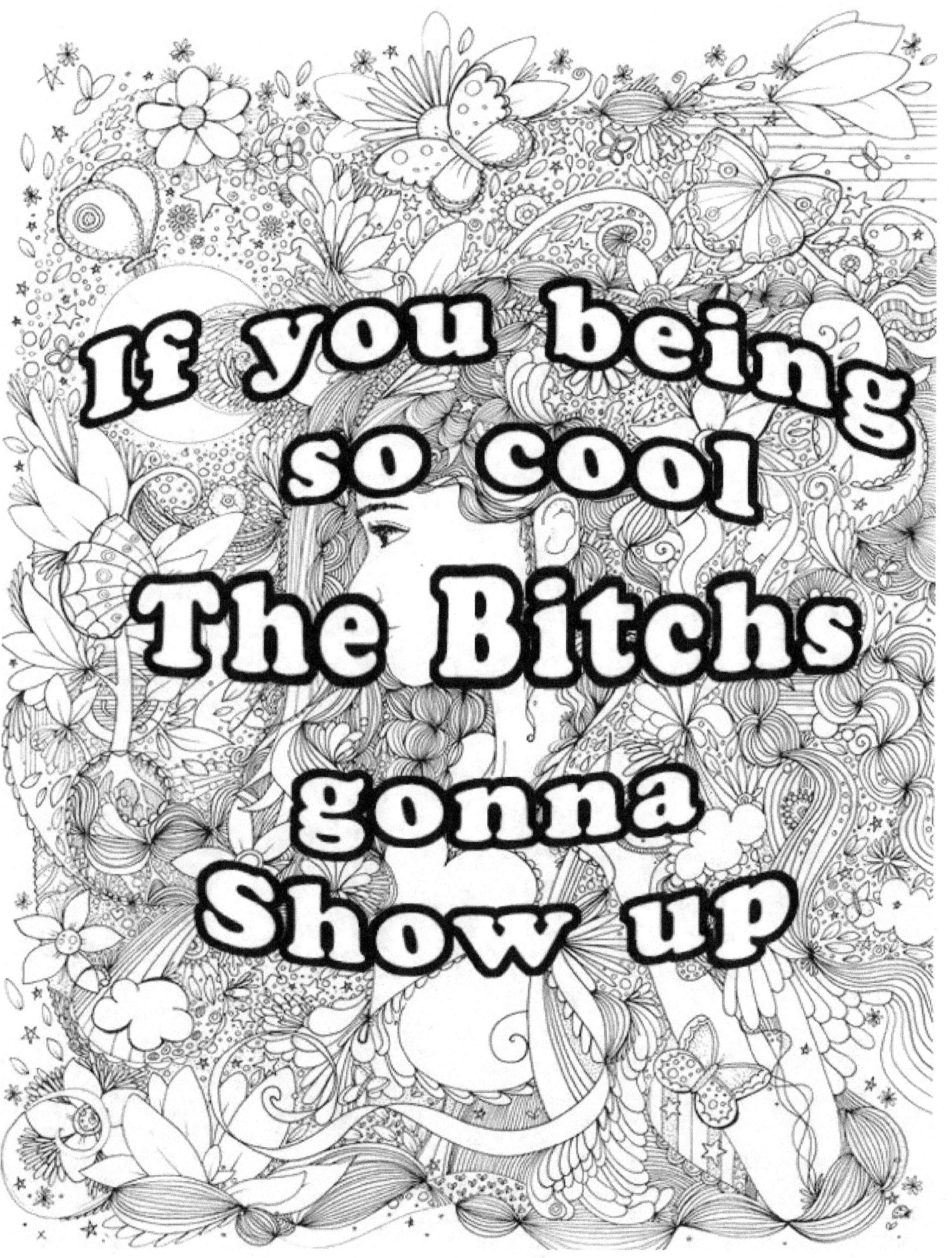

If you being so cool The Bitchs gonna Show up

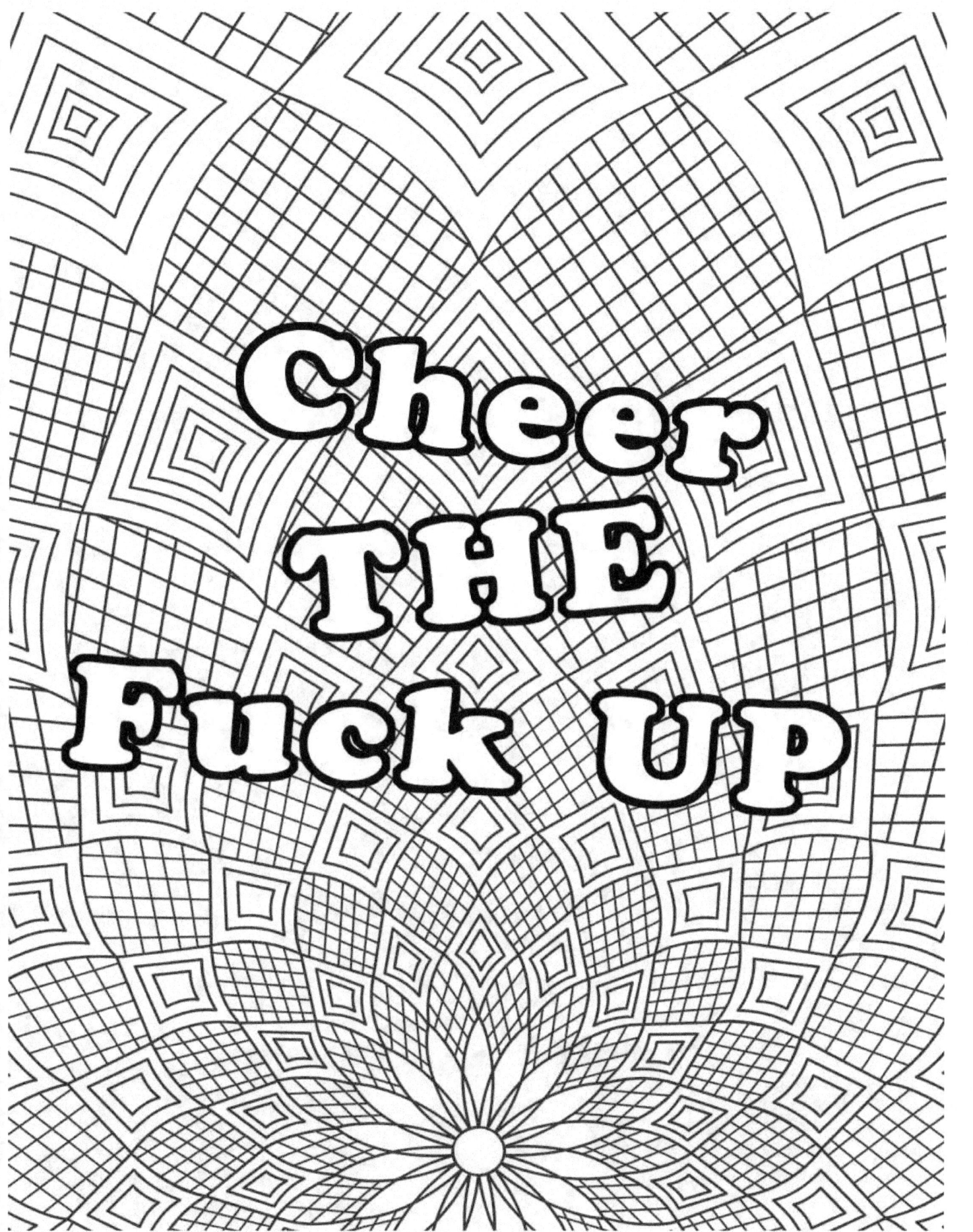

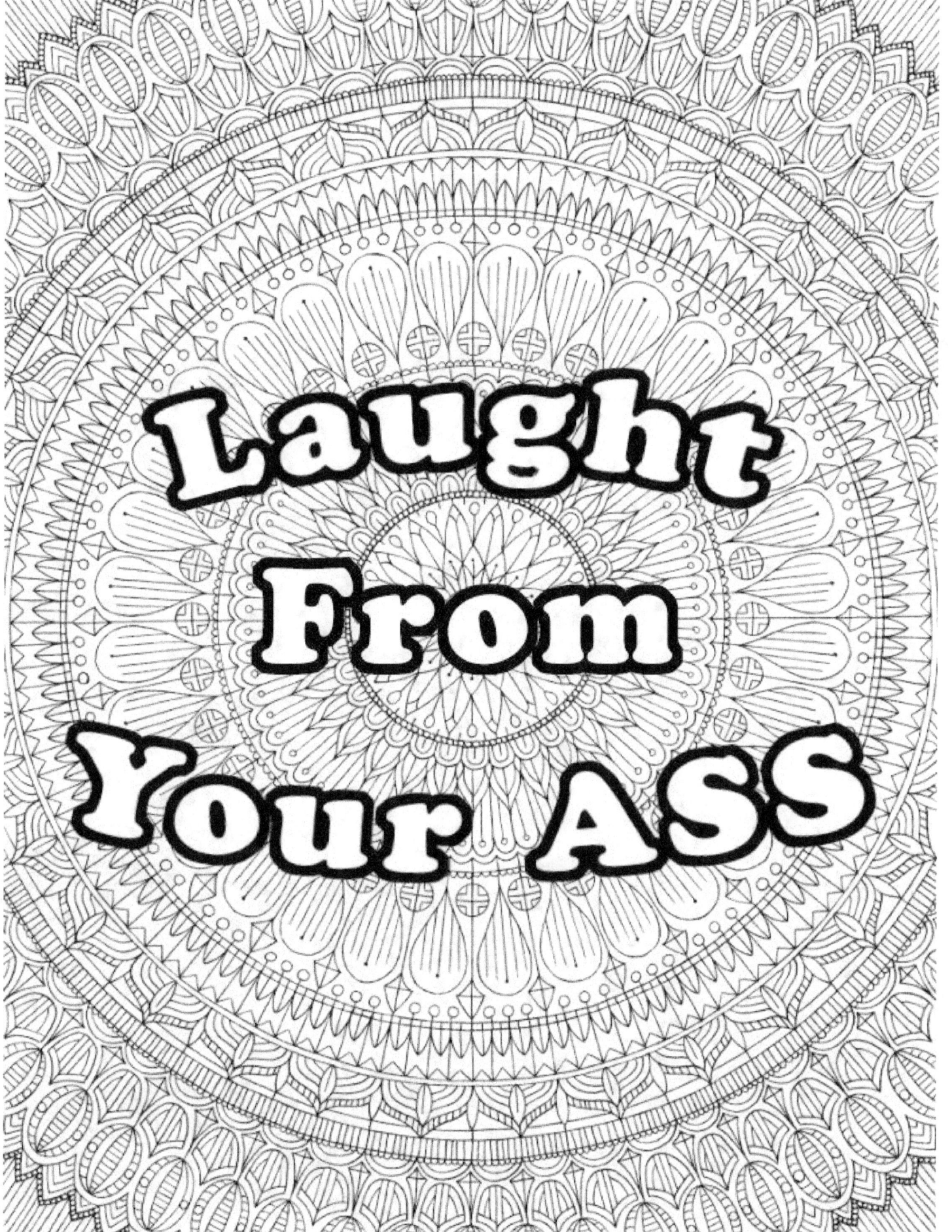

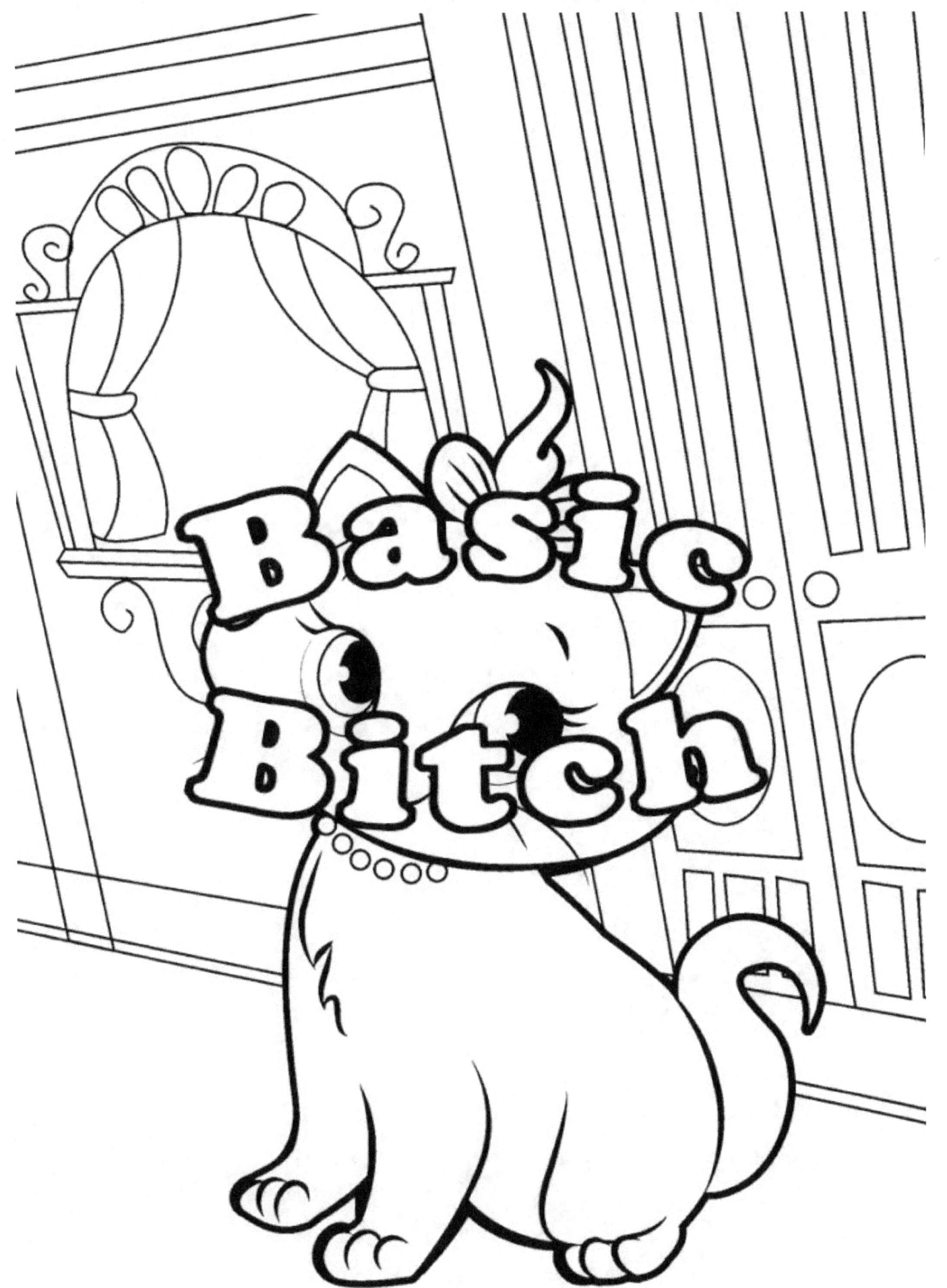

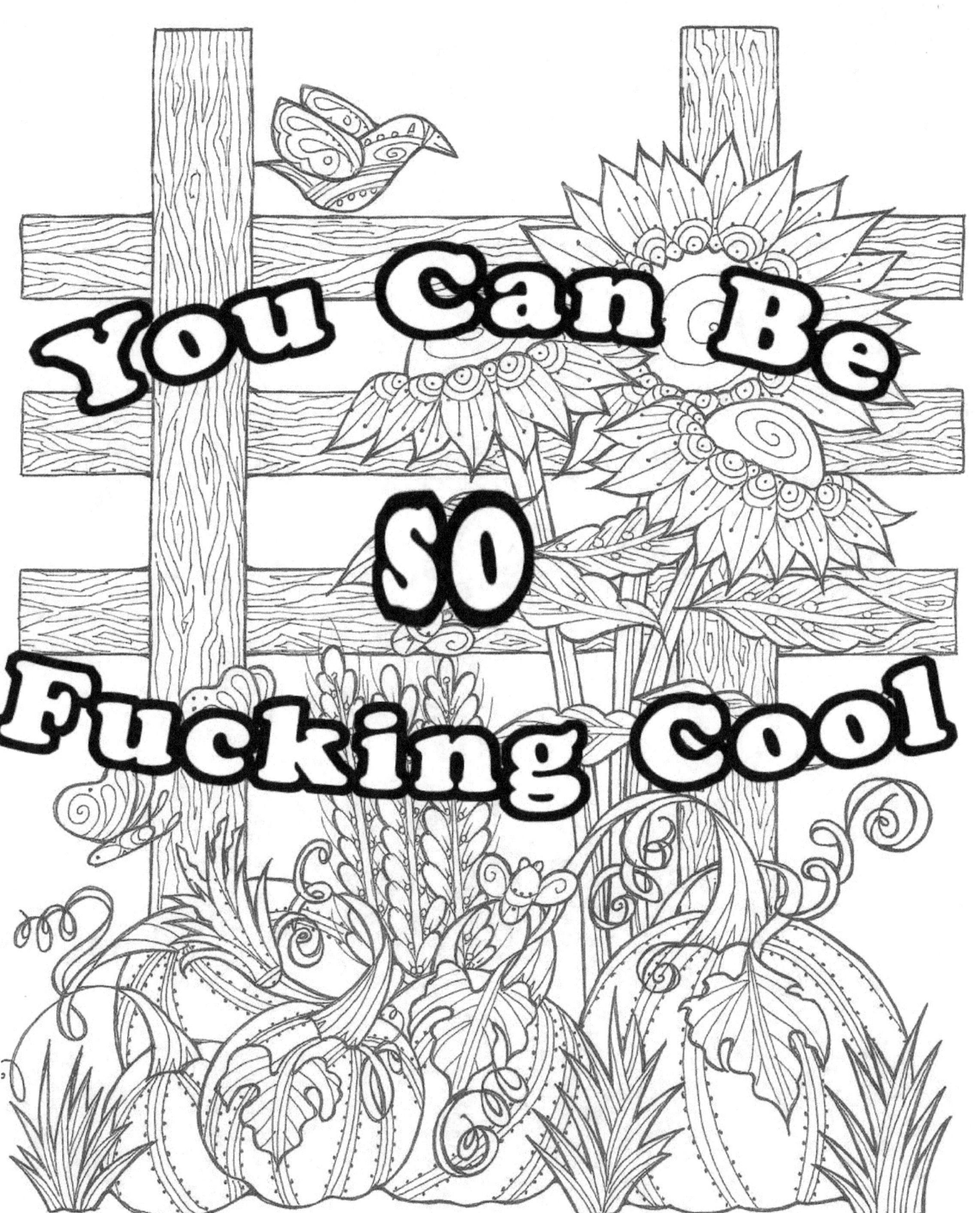

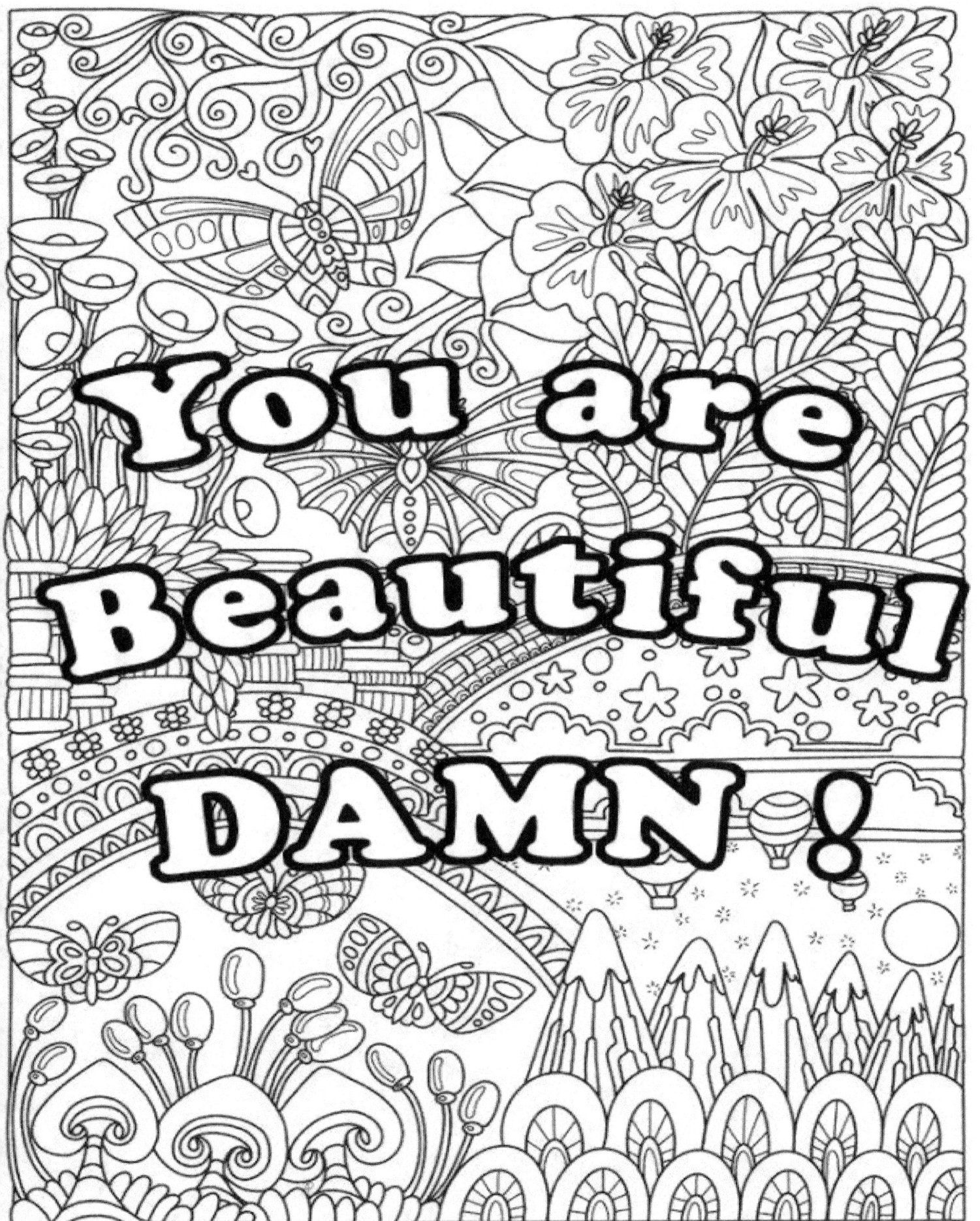

You are Beautiful DAMN!

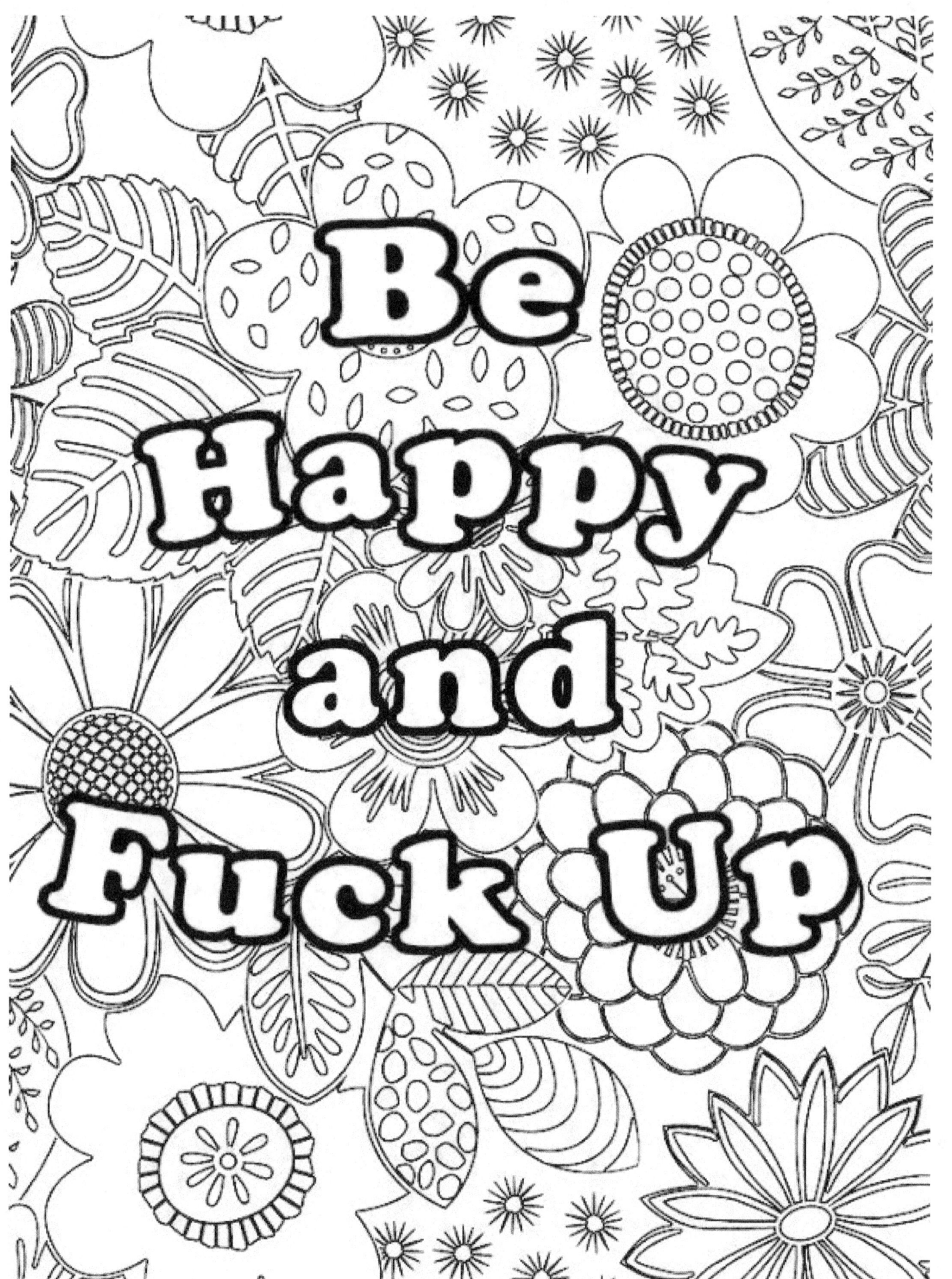

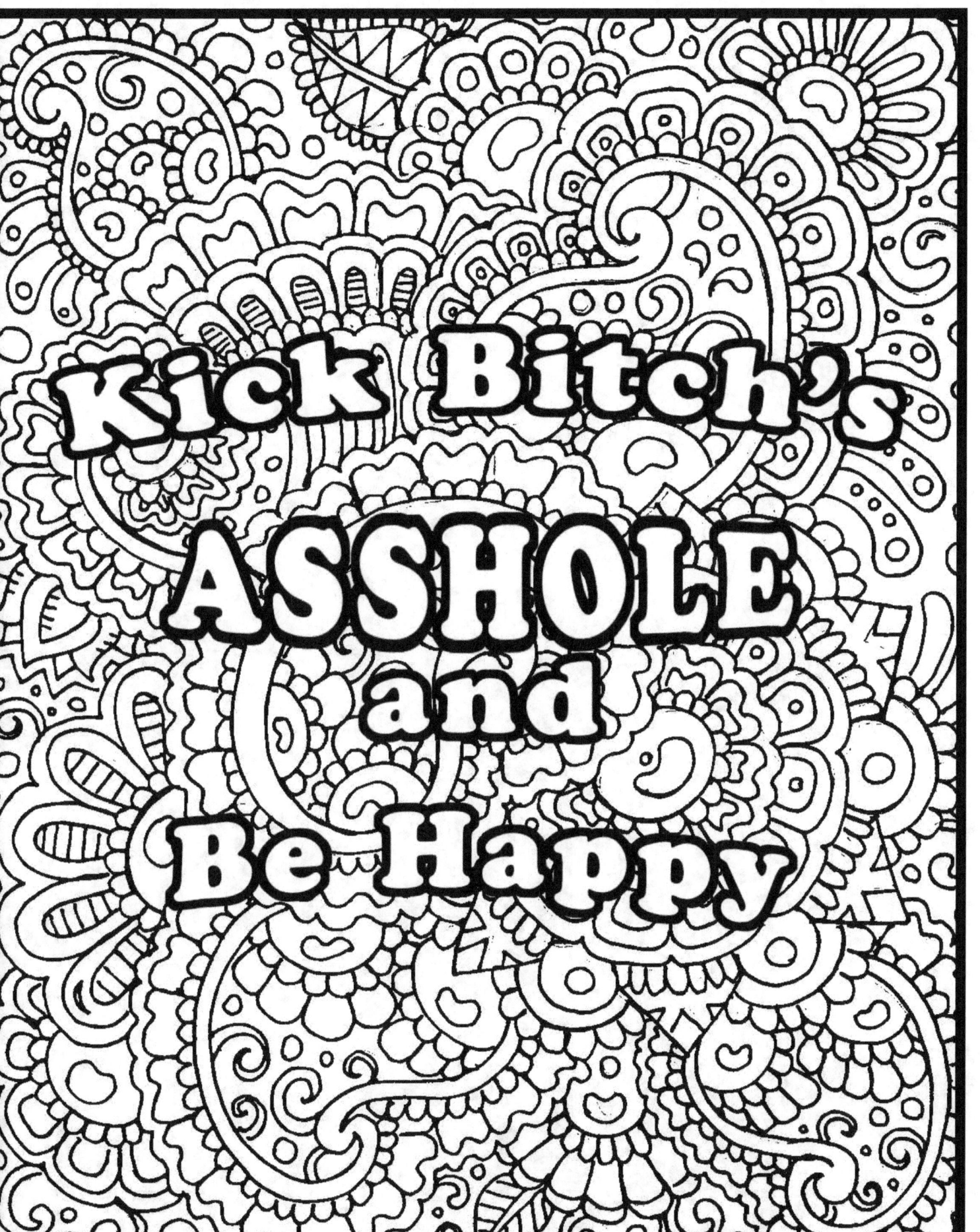

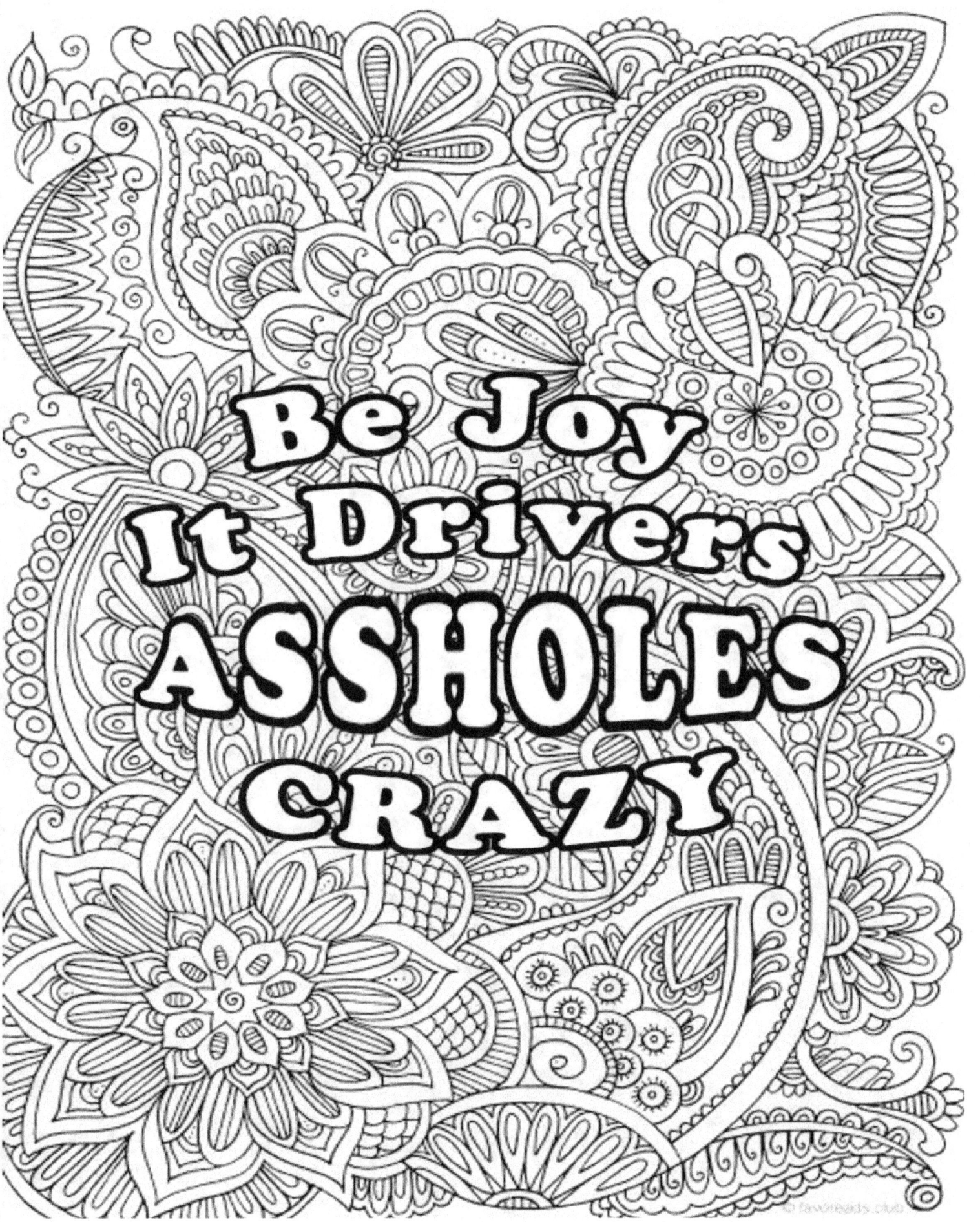

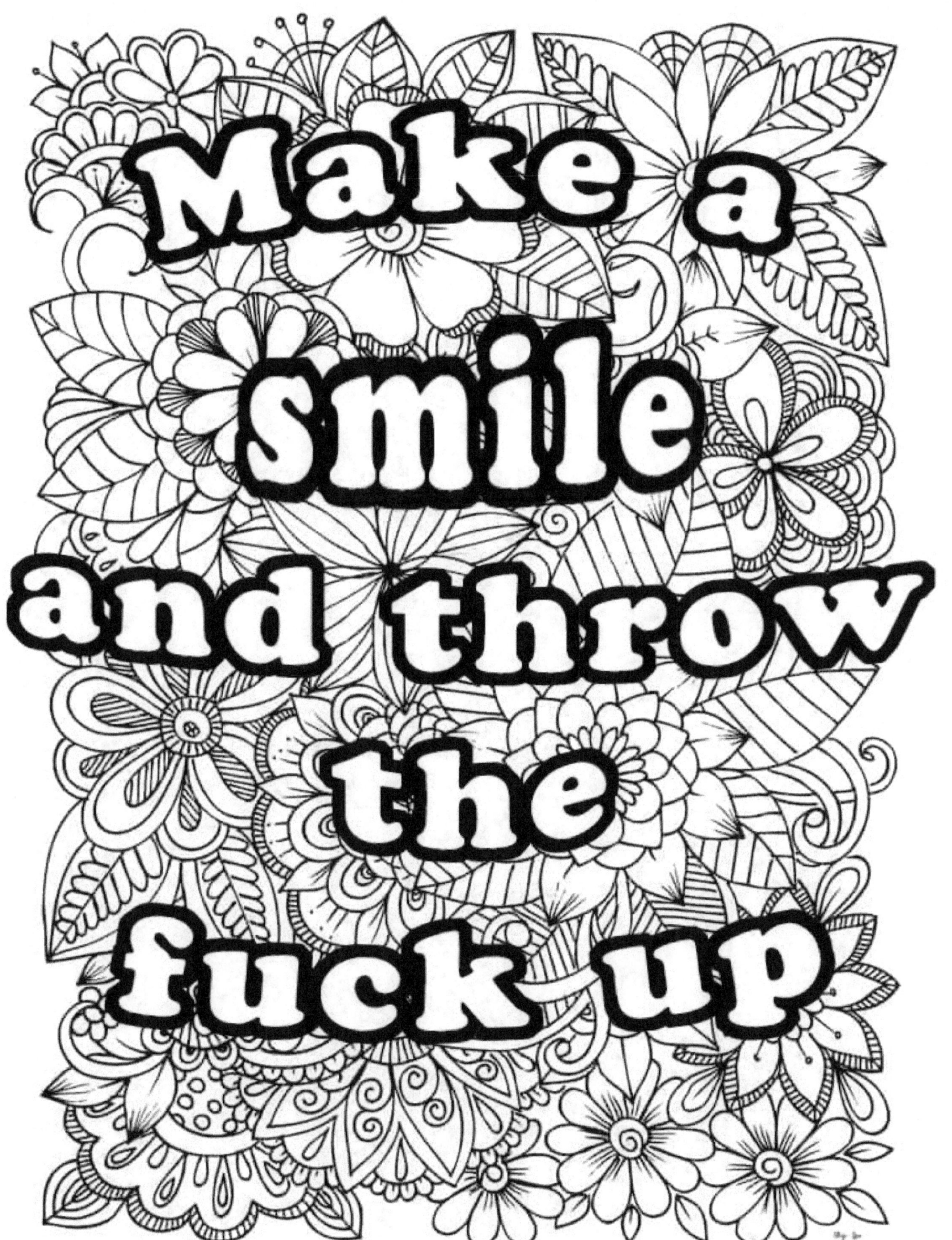

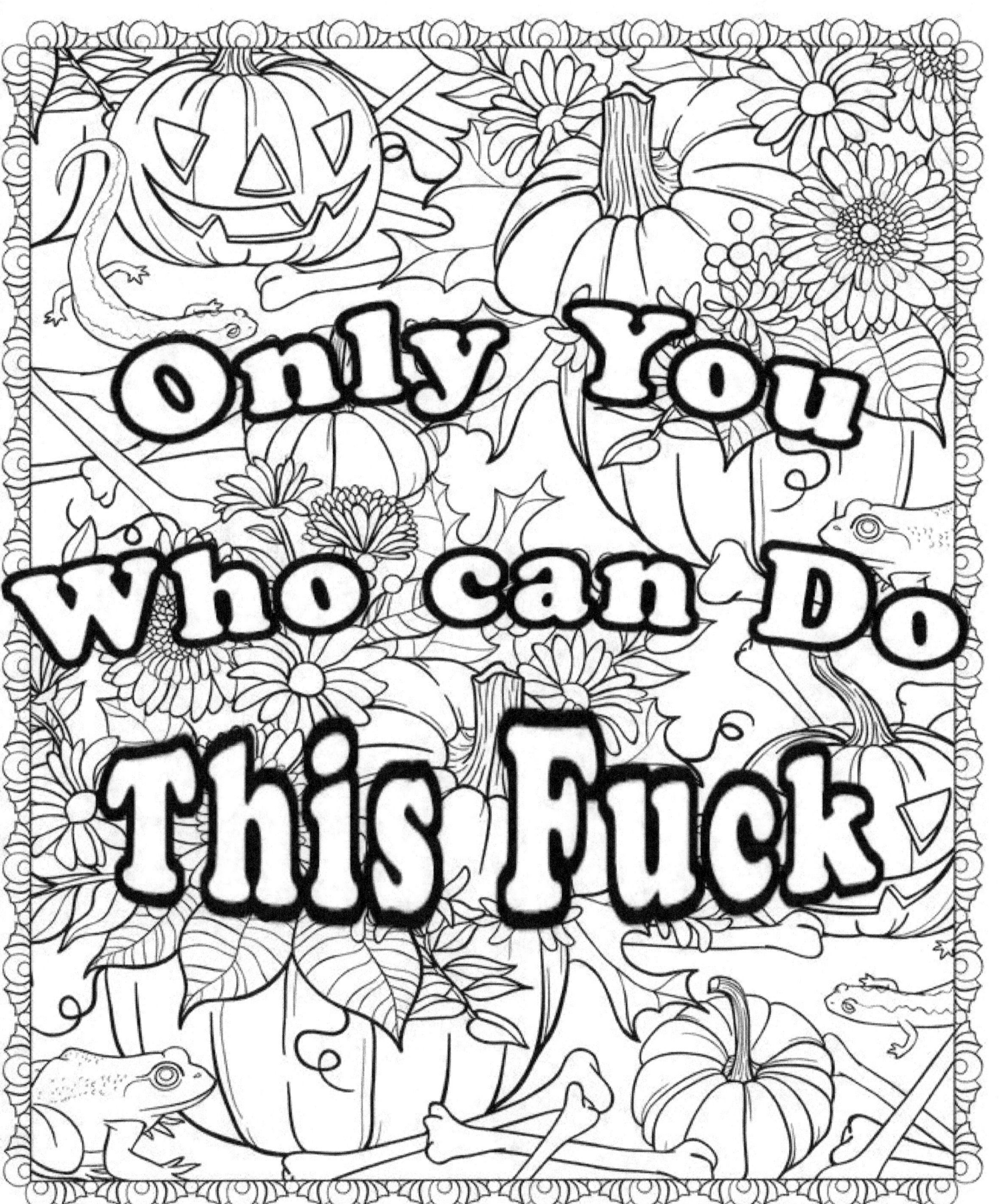

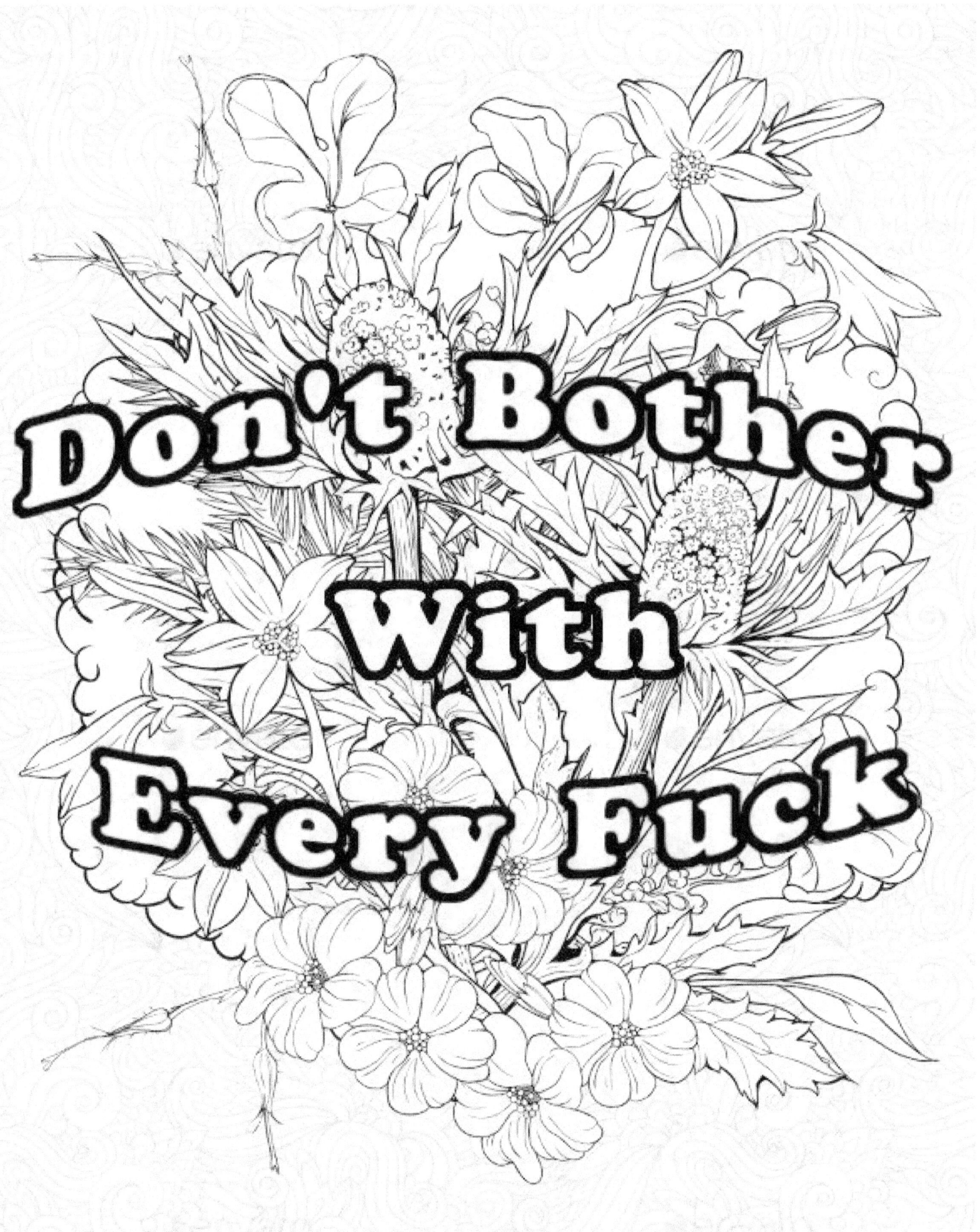

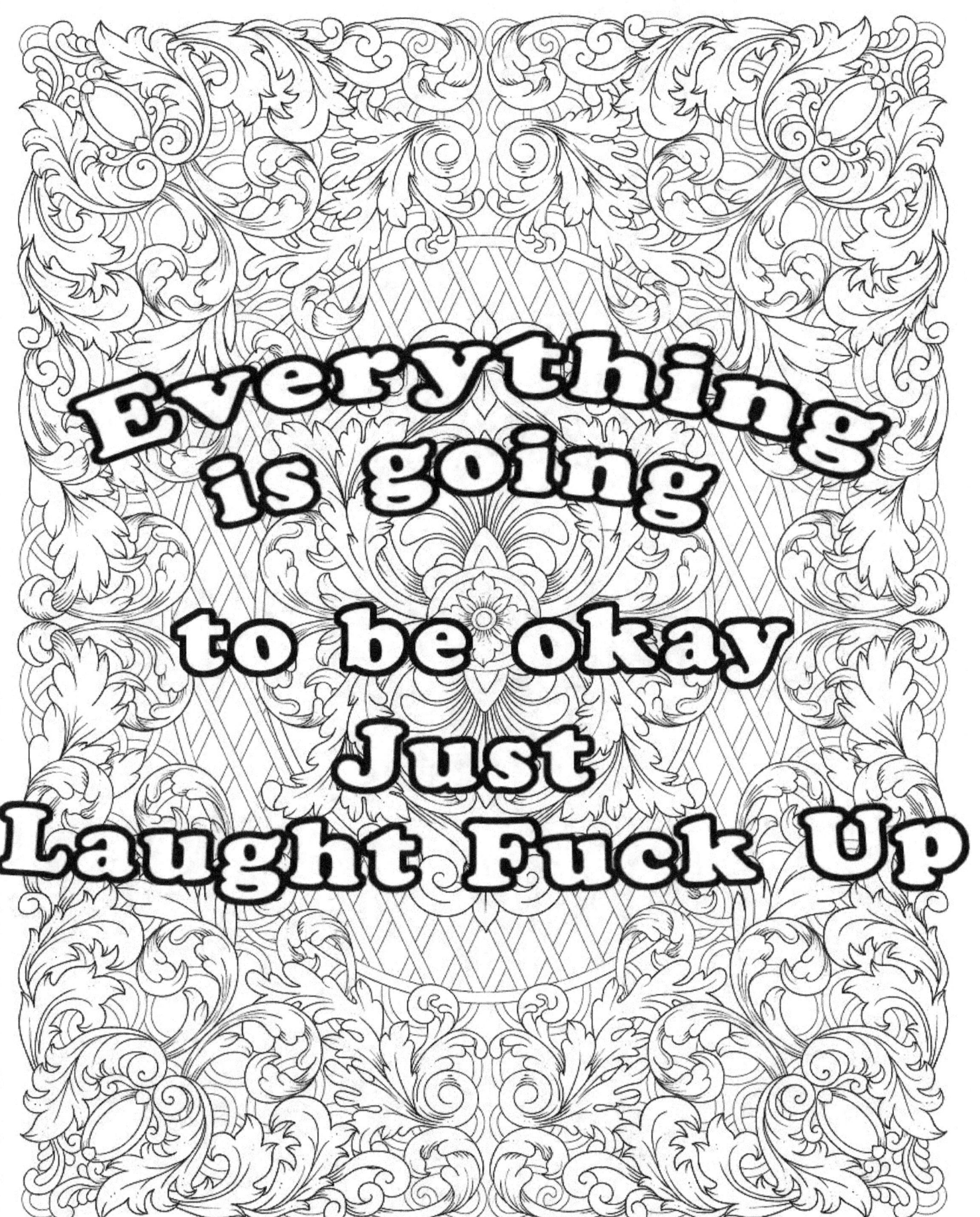

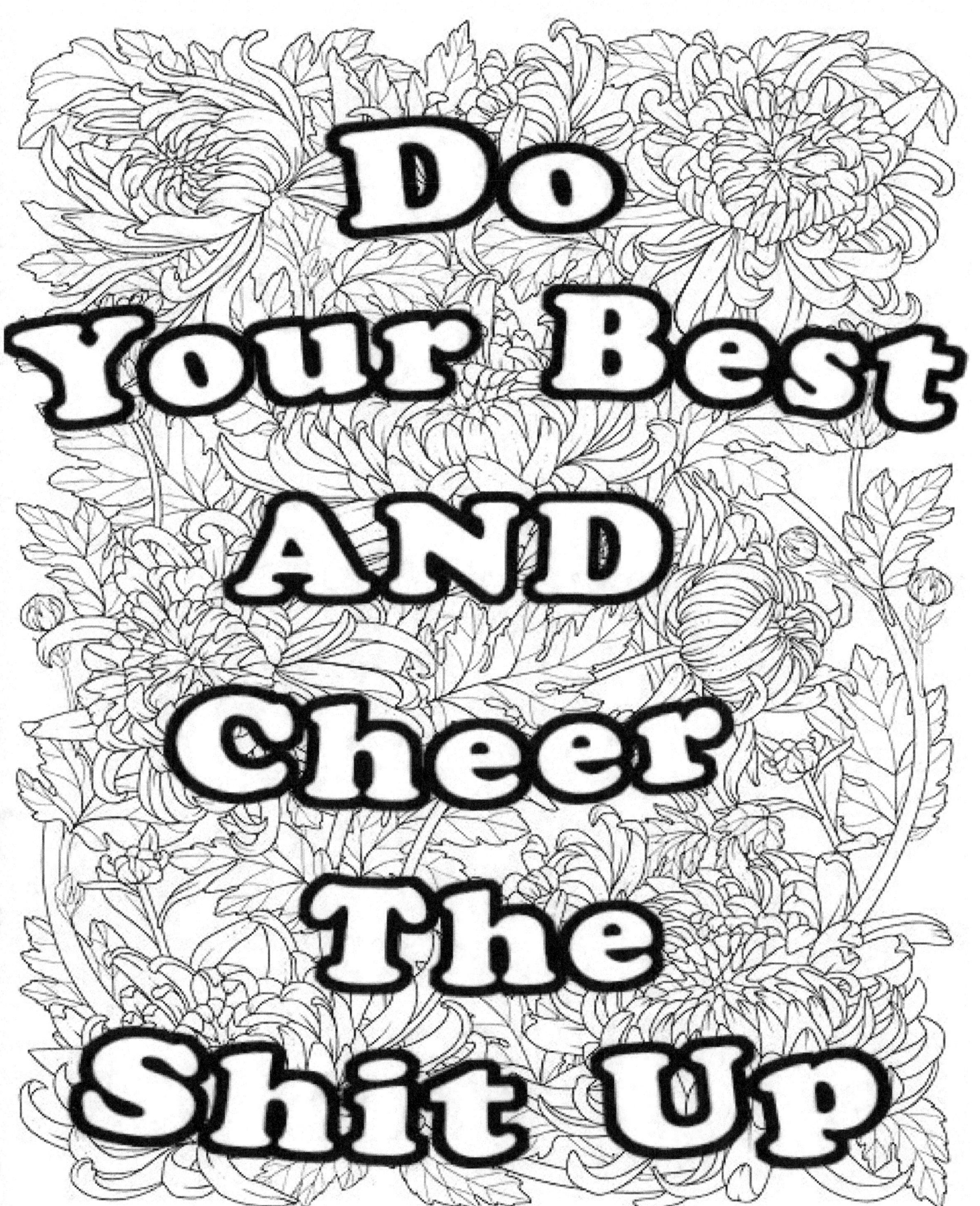

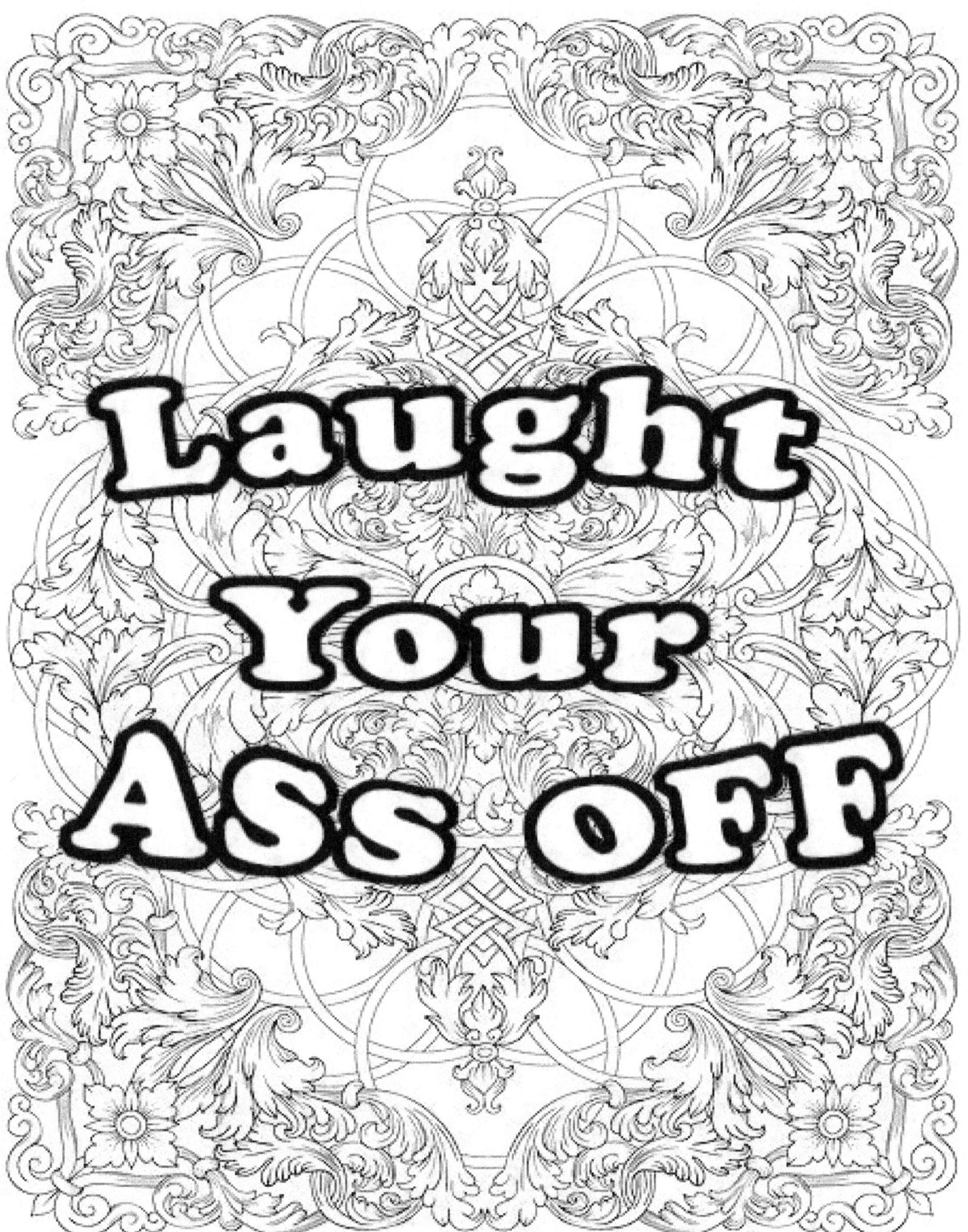

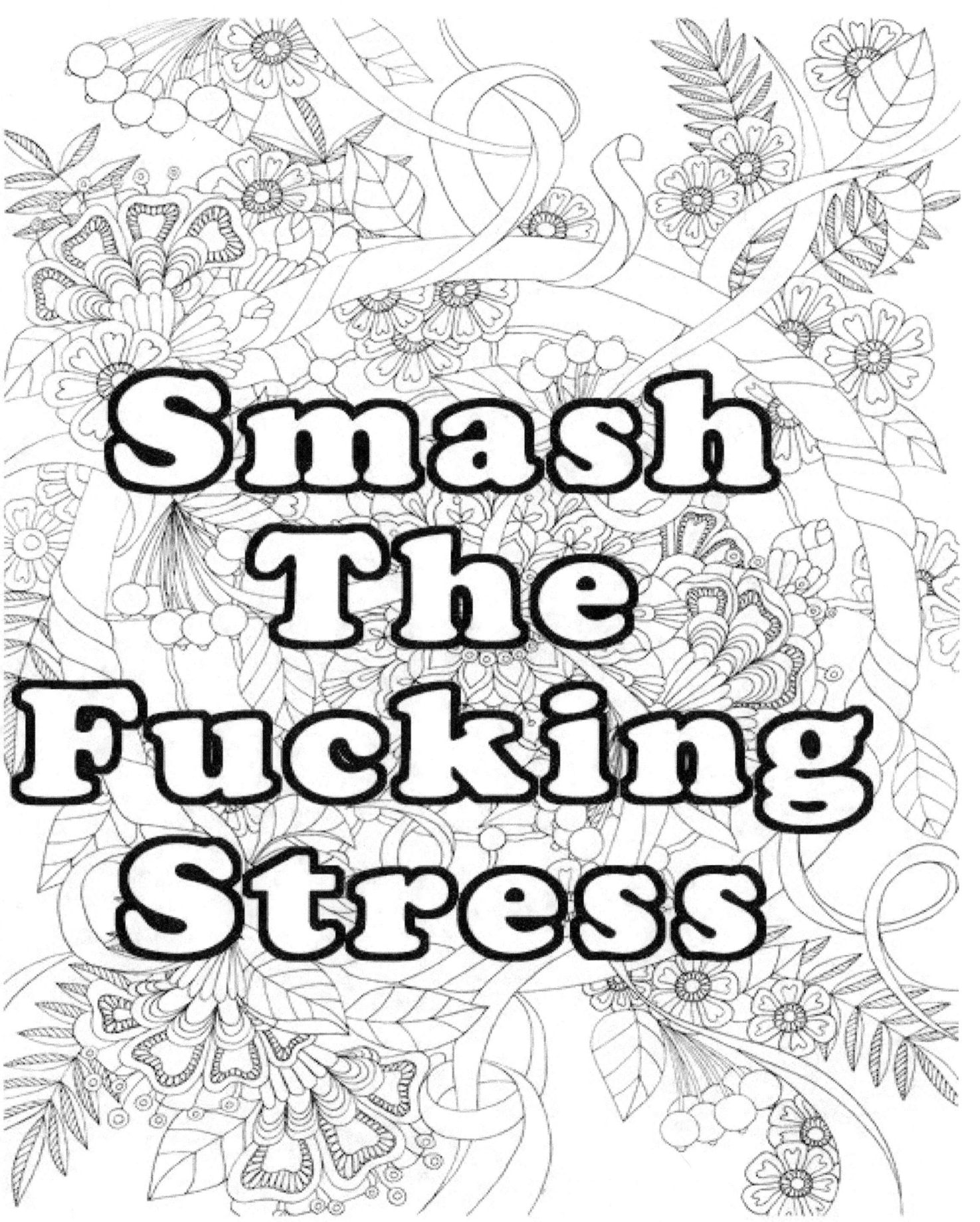

Smash The Fucking Stress

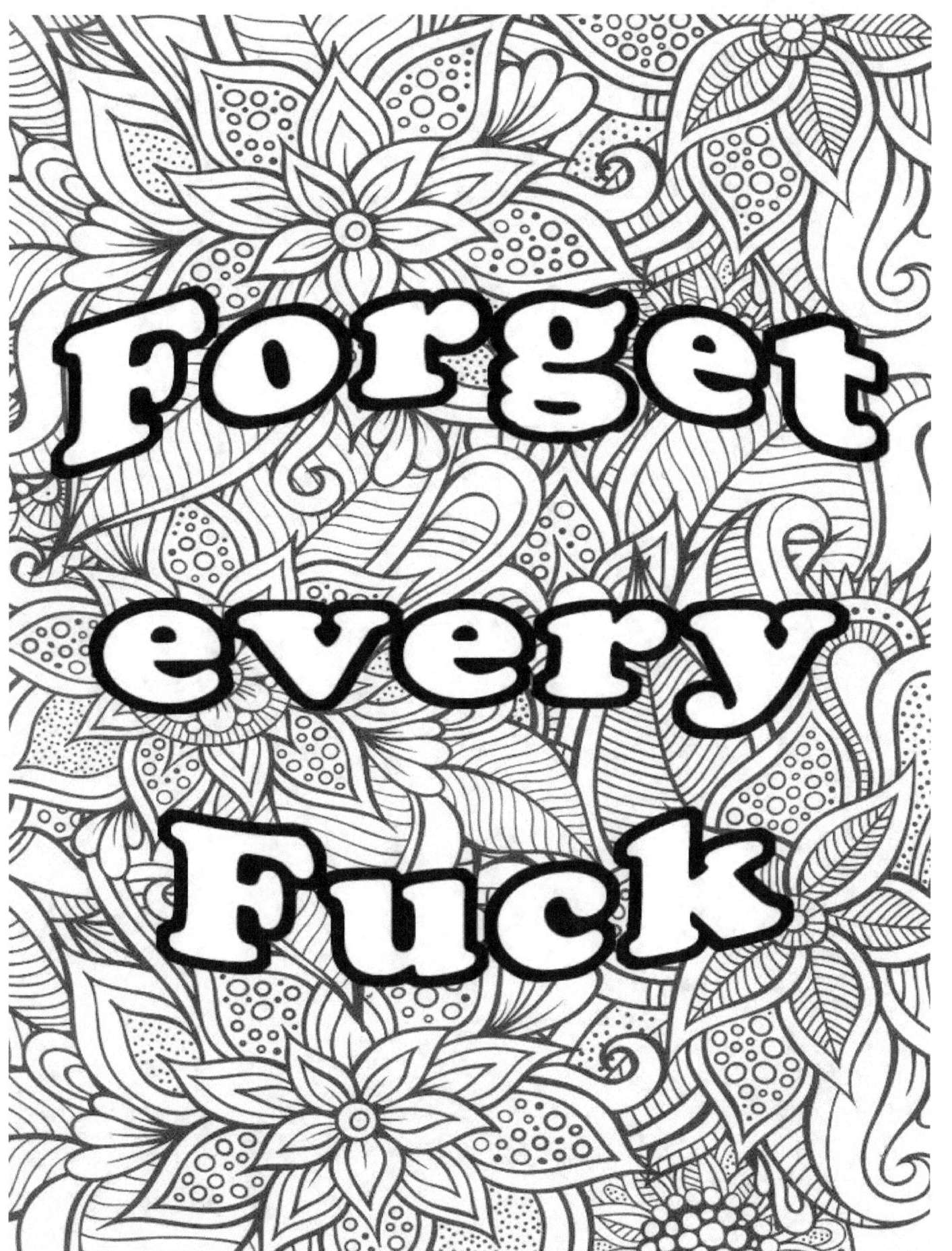

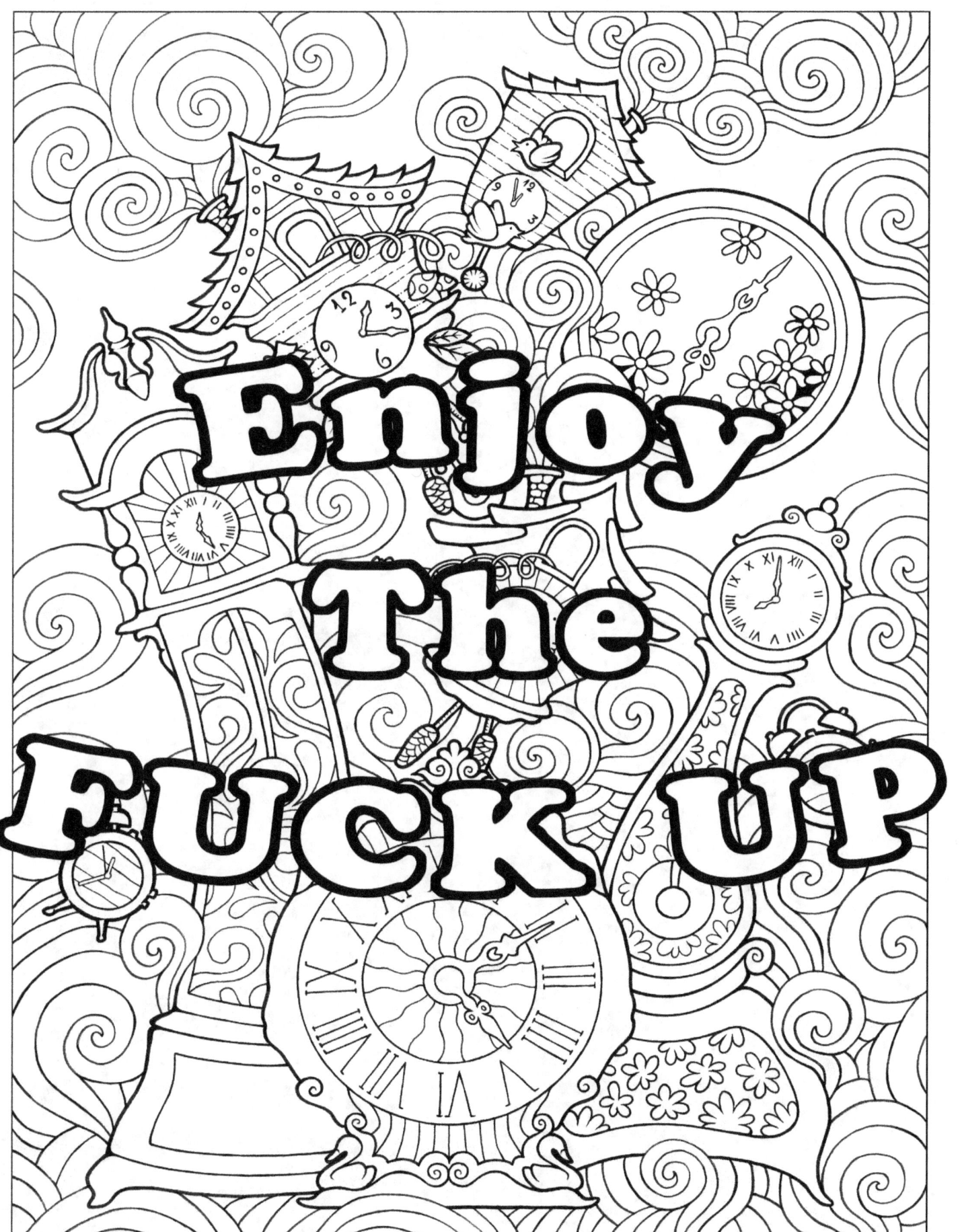

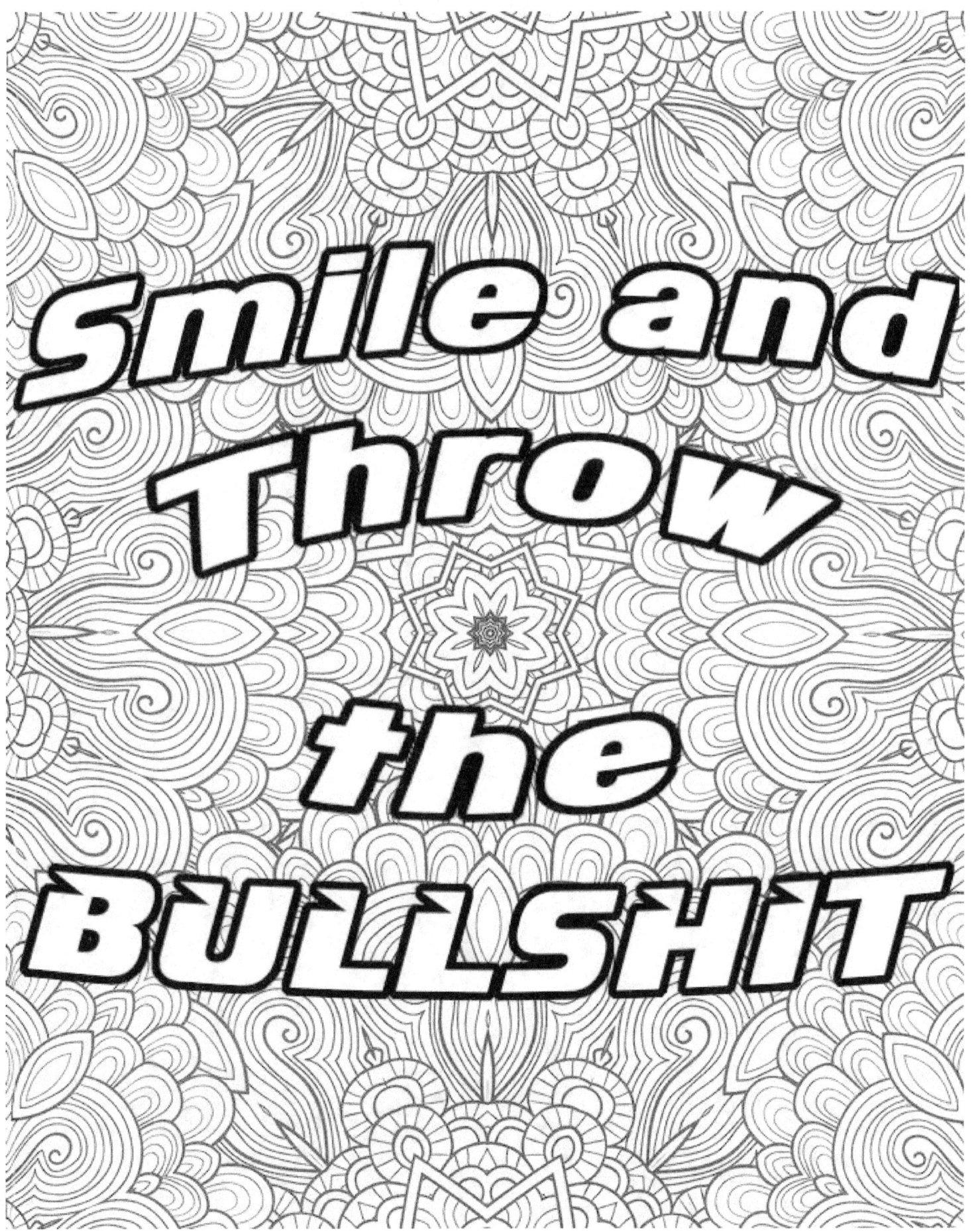

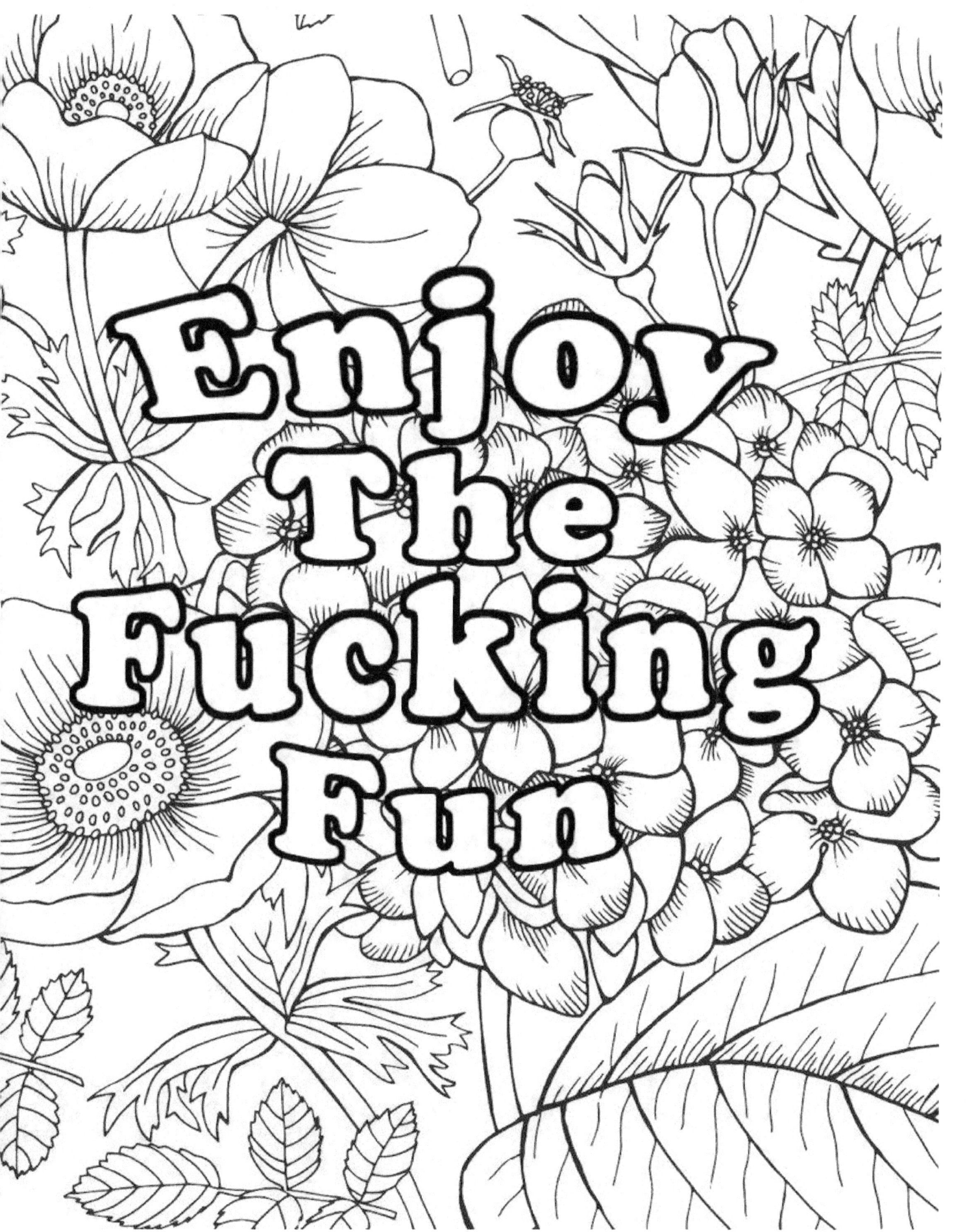

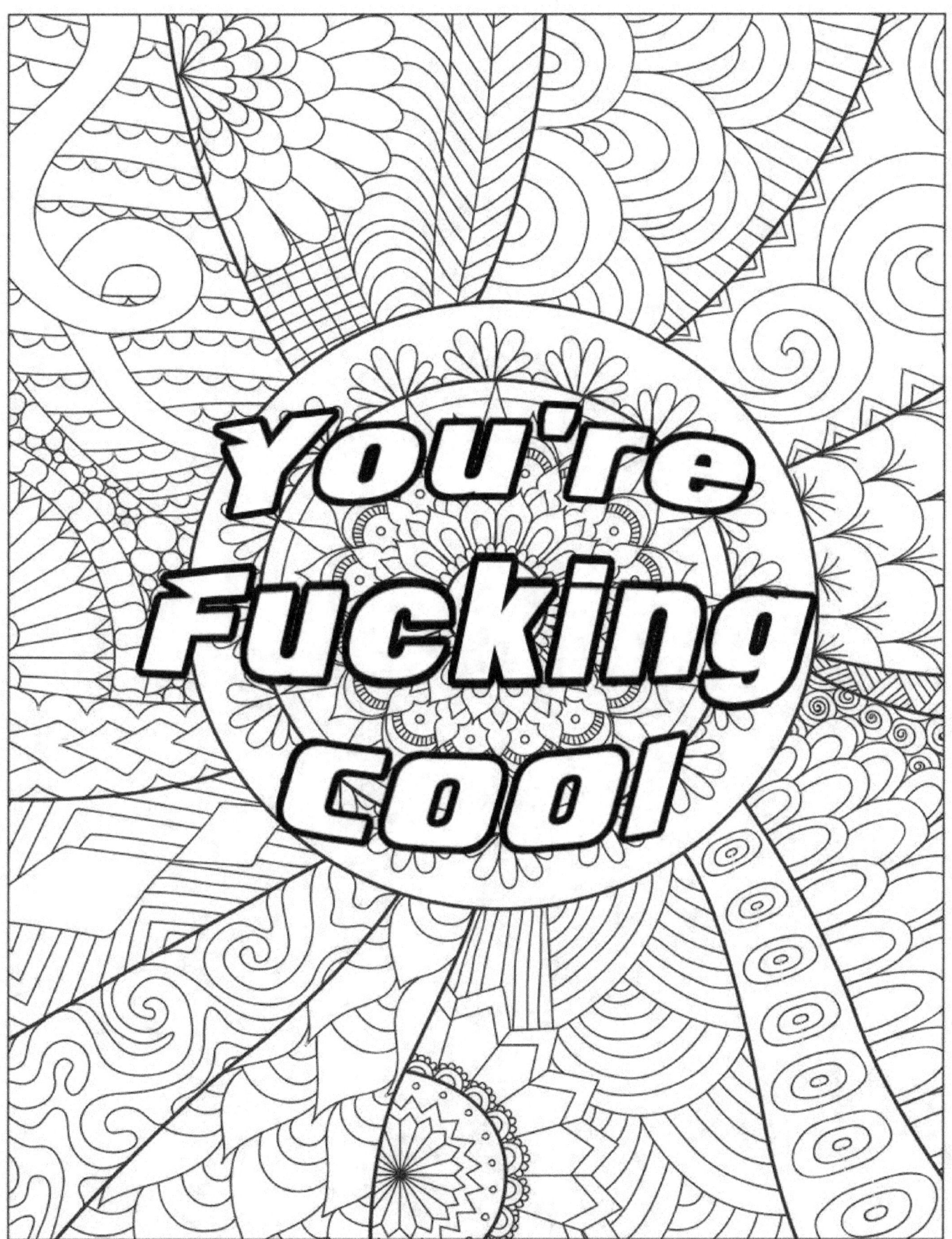

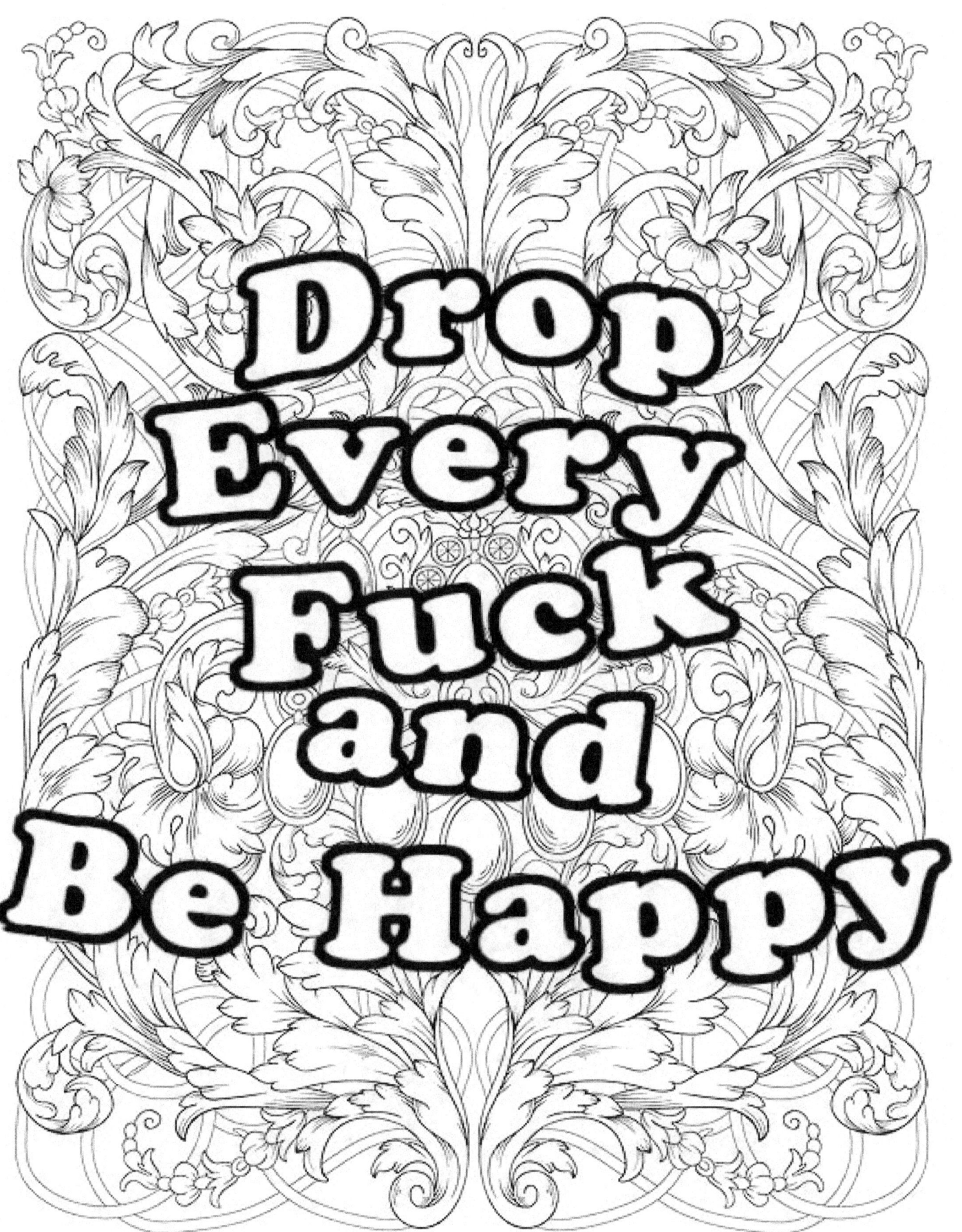

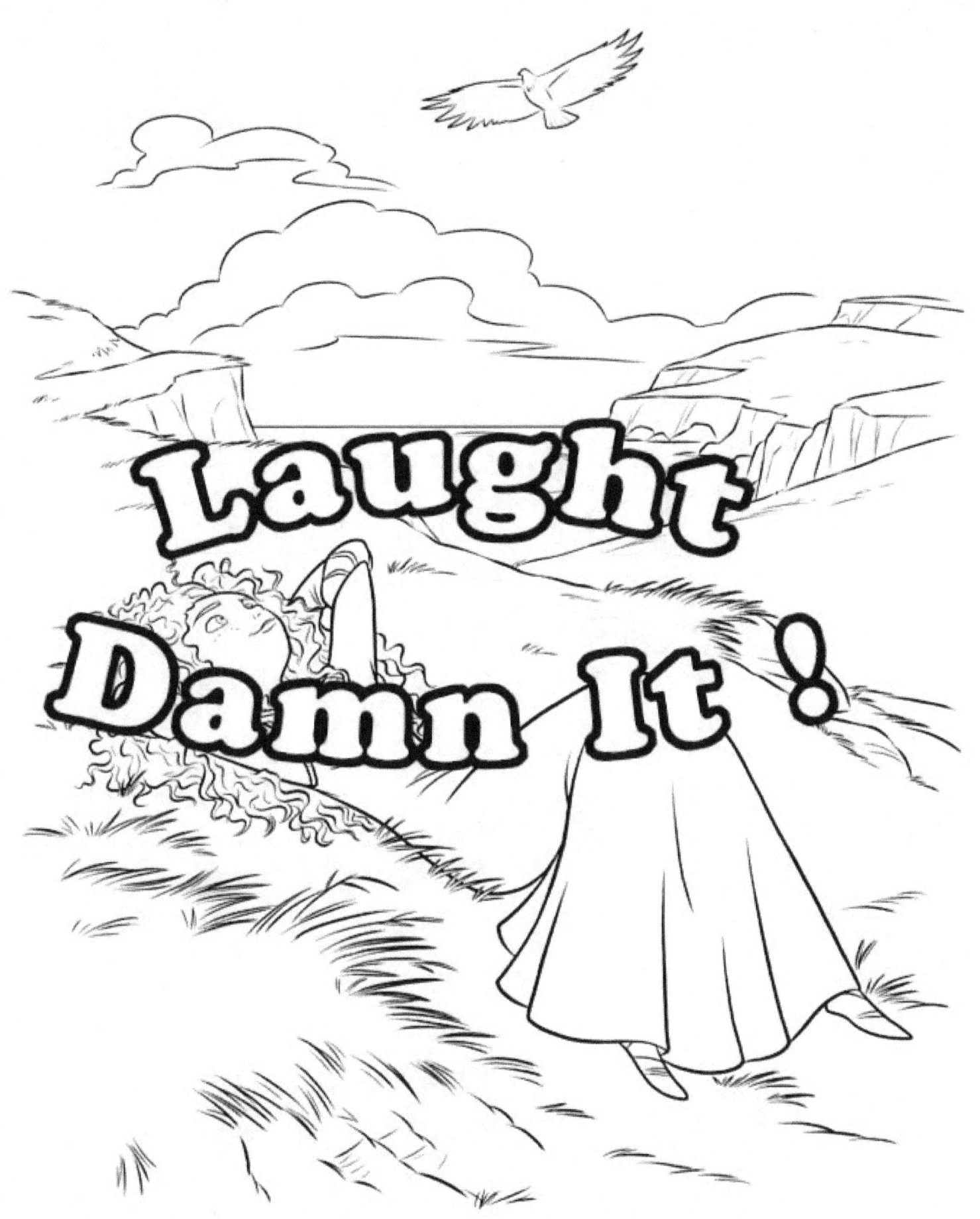

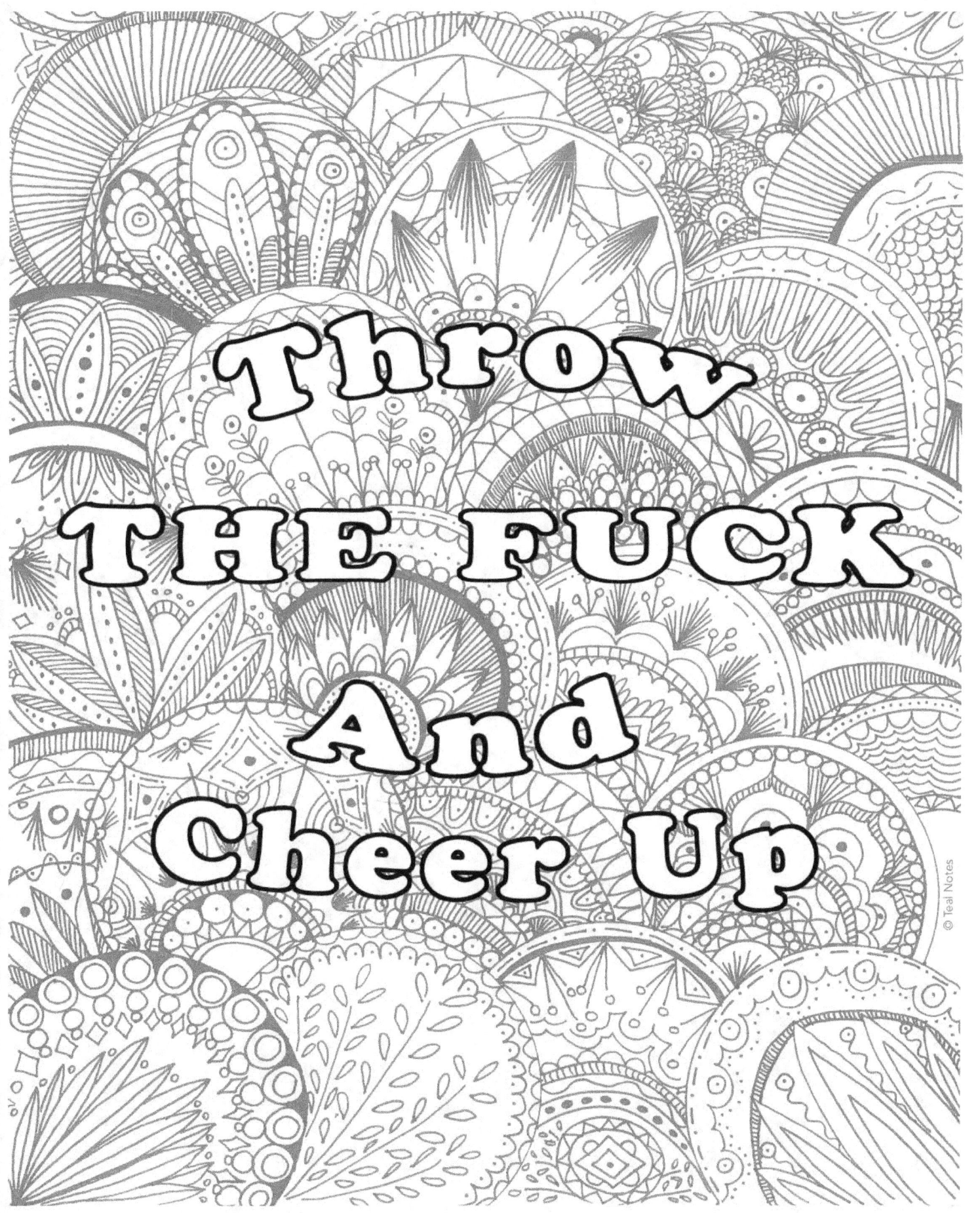

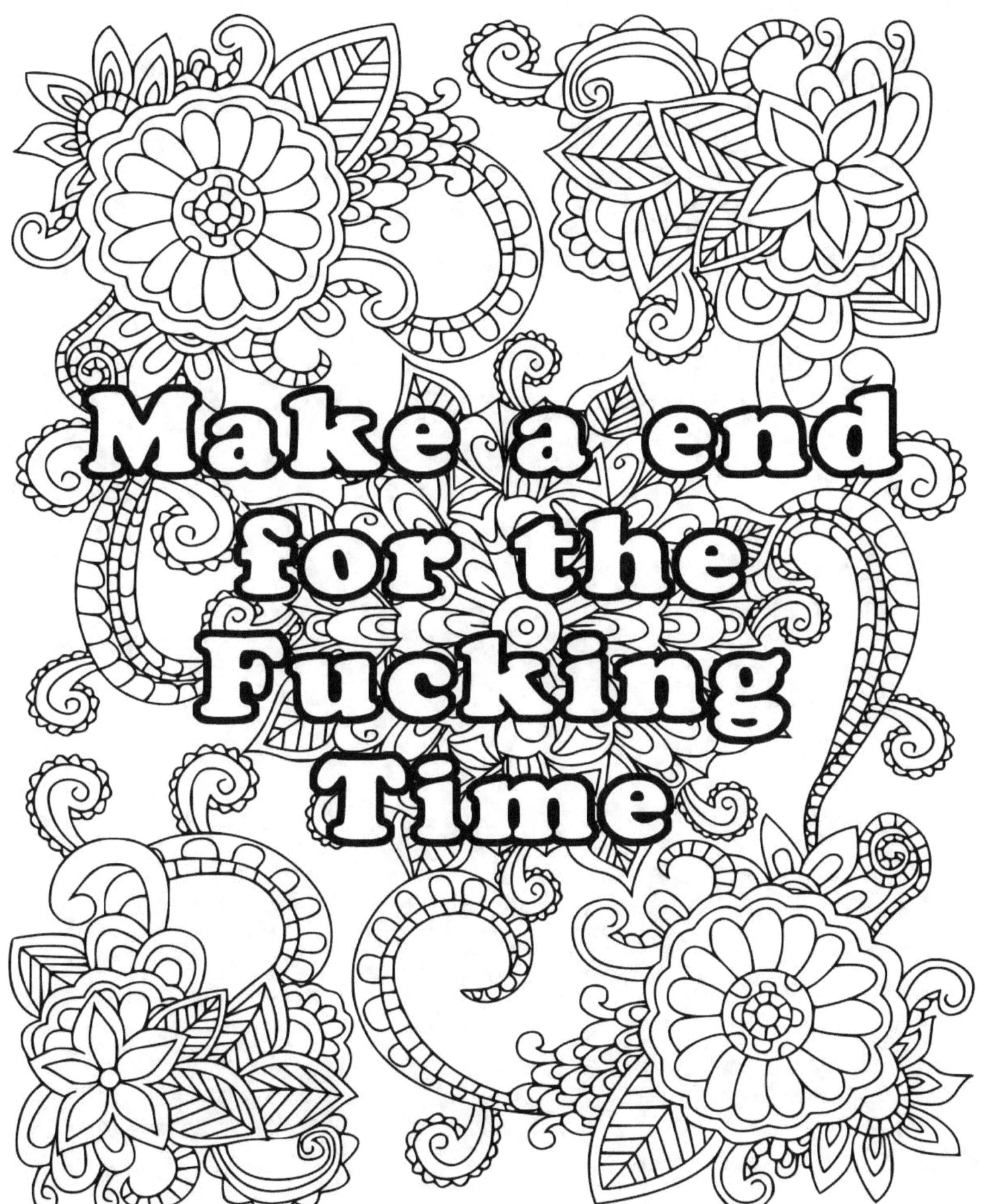

Make a end for the Fucking Time

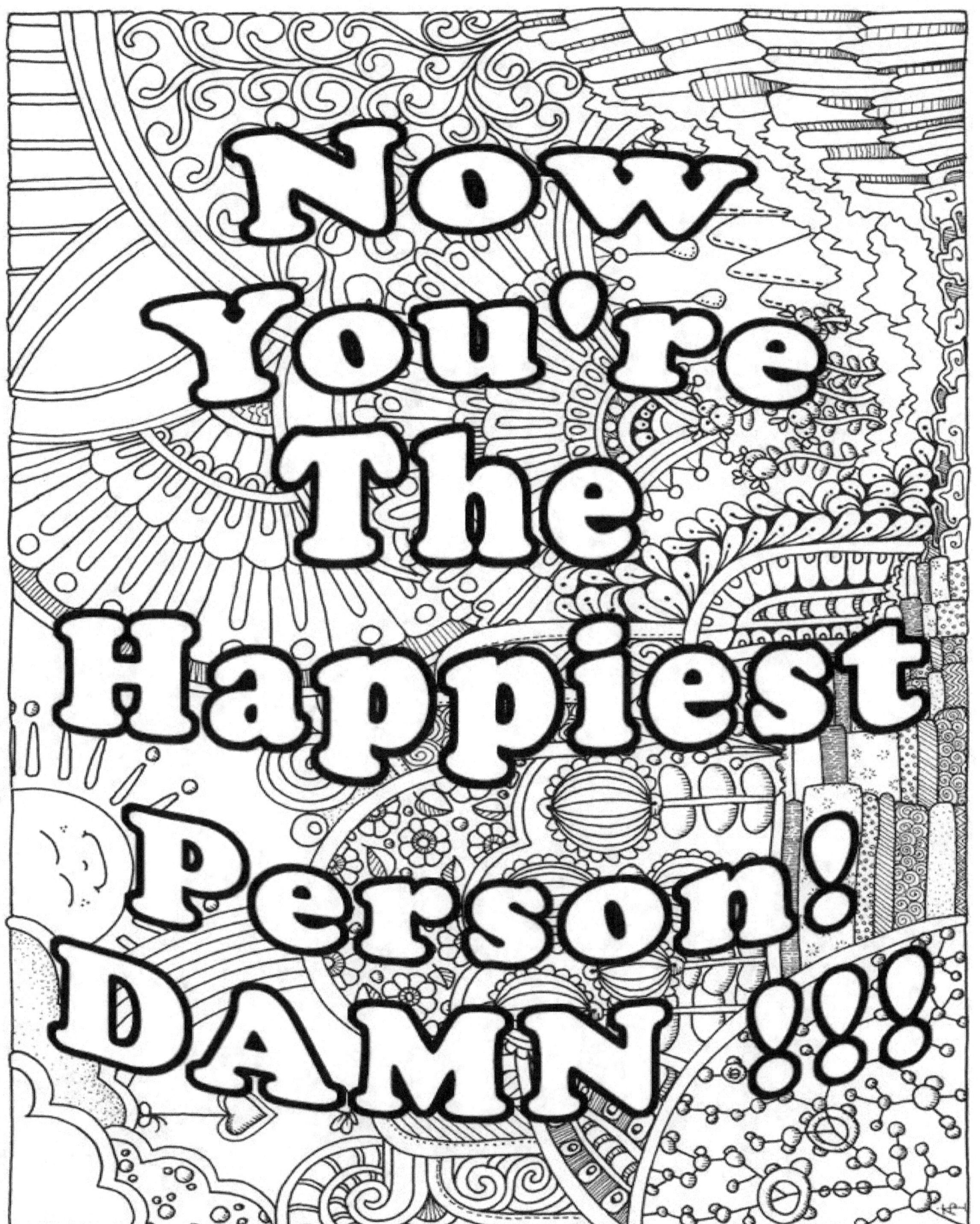

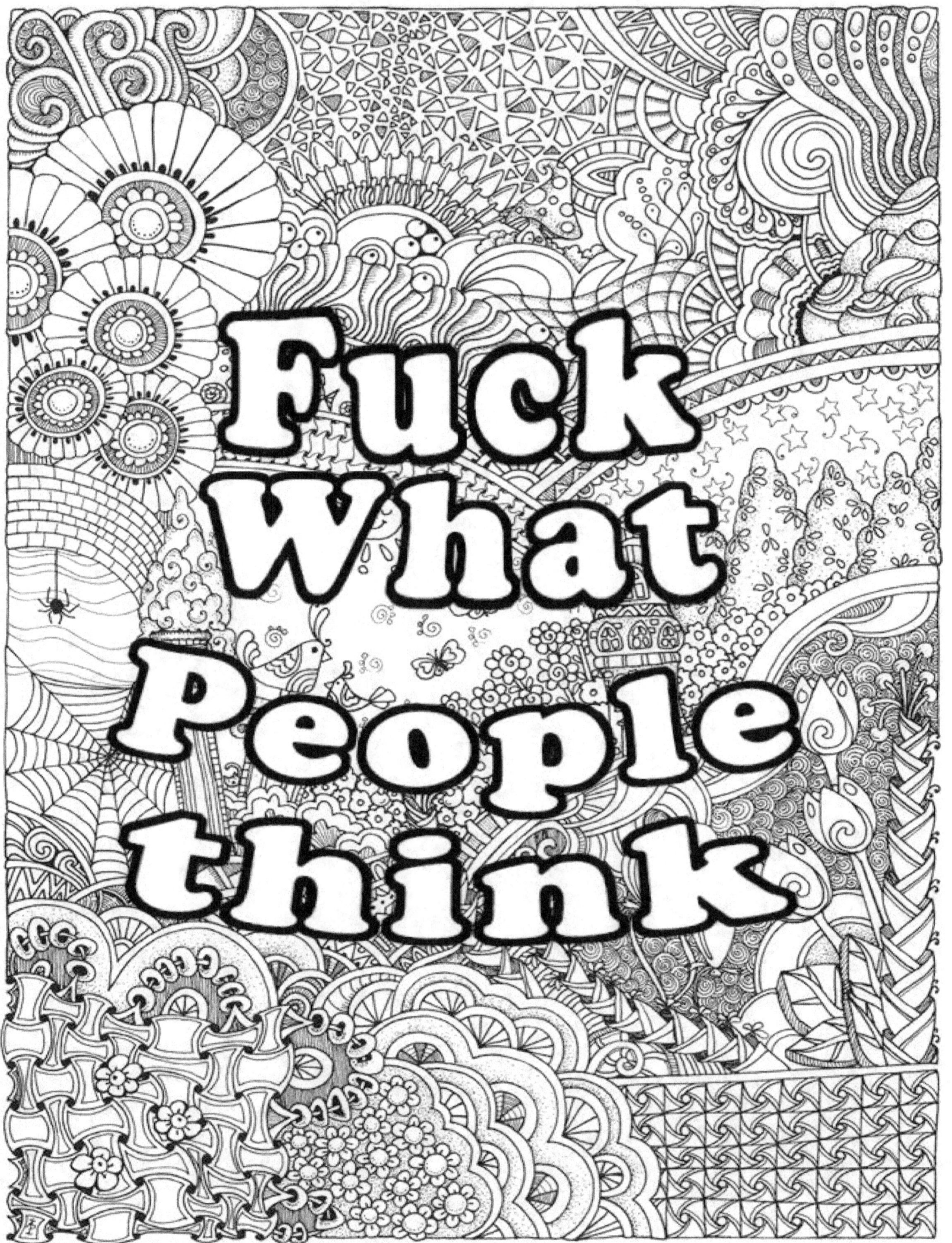

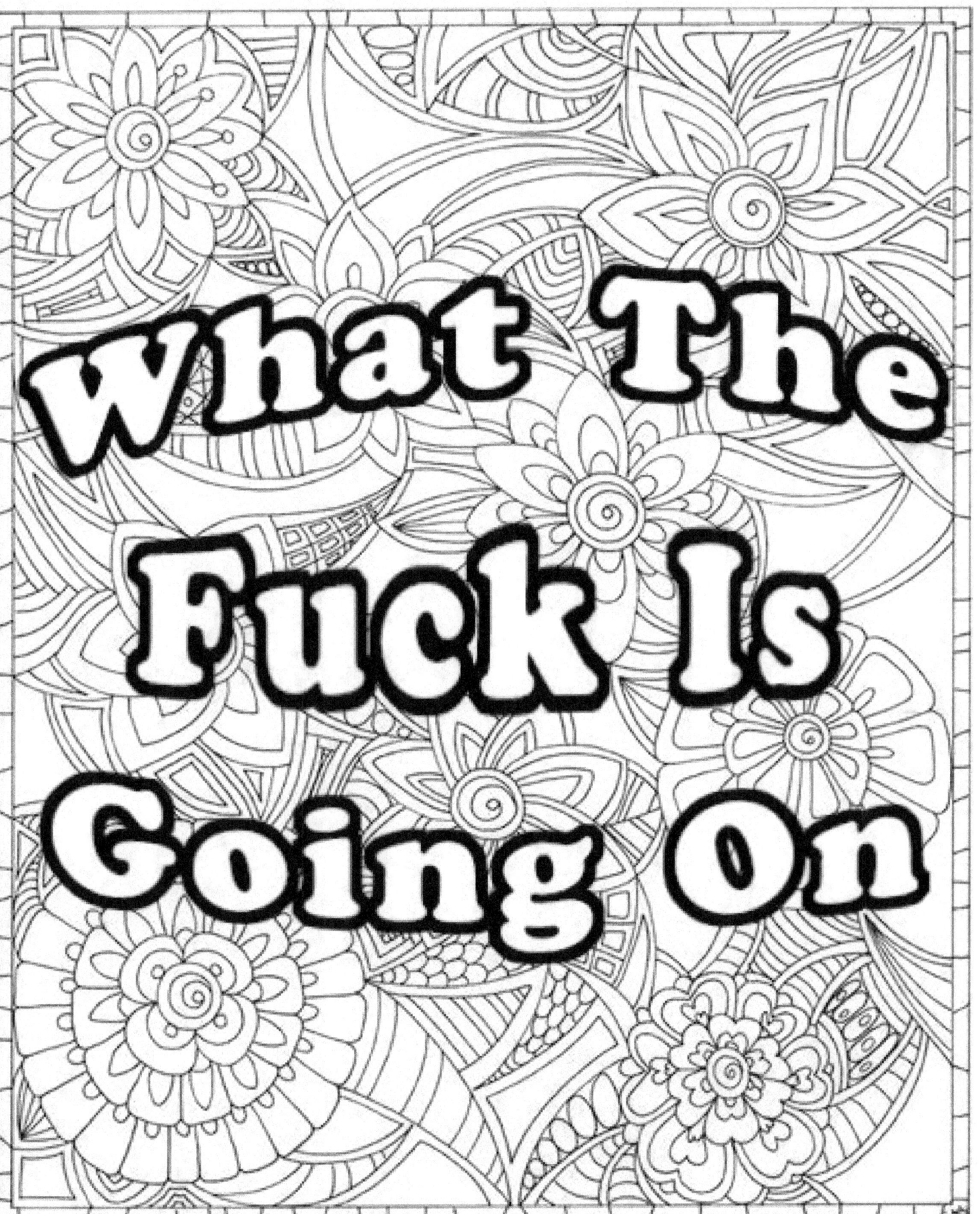